A Child's First Library of Learning

Insect World

TIME-LIFE BOOKS • ALEXANDRIA, VIRGINIA

Contents

❓ Where Can We See Insects?

ANSWER We see insects everywhere we look. They are on the ground, on the water and in the sky.

Here are some common insects and other small animals we can look for. All adult insects have six legs.

We can also find tiny creatures such as these.

Earthworms are found in the ground.

Spiders have eight legs.

Snails and slugs live both on land and in the water.

● To the Parent

Insects are the most successful animals on earth. There are over 900,000 known species and thousands still not classified. Spiders have eight legs and just two parts to their bodies (insects have three body parts) and are classed as arachnids. Snails and slugs are classed as mollusks. Most earthworms are tiny animals, but some can be 11 feet (3.4 m) long!

❓ Why Do Butterflies Like Flowers?

ANSWER There is nectar in flowers. Butterflies go to the flowers to get the nectar. Part of their mouth is like a long tube. They use it like a straw to suck the nectar out of the flowers.

The nectar is way down here.

⁇ Do Insects Visit Flowers Only to Get Nectar?

Some insects don't drink nectar.

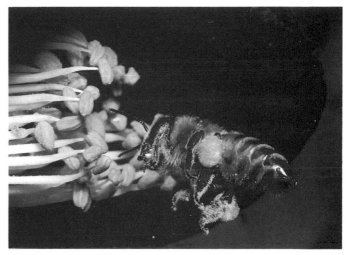

▲ Bees collect nectar and pollen.

▲ Some beetles eat flower pollen.

▲ Mantises catch insects that come to the flowers.

● **To the Parent**

Some insects search out flowers to collect nectar or to gather pollen. Mantises go there to prey on those insects. When the insects come in contact with flowers, pollen sticks to their body and they transfer it to the flowers' pistils, resulting in pollination. In some fruit orchards, bees are kept solely to pollinate the blossoms so that the trees will bear fruit.

How Far Does a Butterfly Fly?

ANSWER Butterflies fly from one flower to another. But some butterflies go a lot farther. Like birds they fly south when the weather is cold. They spend the winter in warm places. When spring comes they fly home.

▲ **Monarch butterfly**

■ **Migration routes**

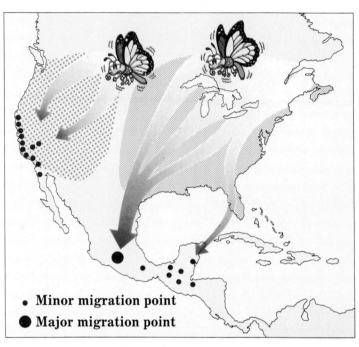

• **Minor migration point**

● **Major migration point**

▲ When migrating butterflies stop for the night their bodies can completely cover the branches of several trees.

Thousands of monarch butterflies resting on a tree trunk for the night appear to be pasted on top of one another. ▶

❓ Why Do Moths Fly Around Lights?

(ANSWER) When moths fly at night they are attracted by light. As they fly nearer the source of the light, it seems stronger in one eye than it does in the other. They keep turning in the direction where they feel the light strongest. That's why they fly toward a light in circles or spirals.

Are Butterflies Also Attracted to Light?

Butterflies do not fly to light like moths. Most butterflies come out only when it is daylight. That is one way you can tell the difference between a moth and a butterfly.

■ Other differences between moths and butterflies

Butterflies rest with their wings standing up, but moths rest with their wings flat.

Most butterflies have bright colors while most moths have dull colors. The antennae of butterflies are swollen at the tips, while those of moths are not.

 TRY THIS

On a dark night when there is little wind, put a piece of light cloth or paper near a light. You will find that it attracts moths and other kinds of flying insects.

● **To the Parent**

Nocturnal insects are attracted to light, a response that is called phototaxis. Movement of the wings is influenced by the strength of the light. When the light reaches both eyes with equal intensity, as from a distant source such as the moon, the insect can fly in a straight line with both wings moving the same way. But light coming from a closer source, such as a nearby candle, is perceived more strongly by one eye than by the other. As a result of this the wings on one side are stimulated to move faster, causing the insect to approach the light source in a spiral path and fly right into the light.

❓ How Do Bagworms Become Moths?

ANSWER There is a larva inside this bag made of leaves and twigs. The bag is a nest that protects it. Male larvae turn into moths and fly away in the summer. Females remain as larvae and live in the nest.

▶ This moth is the male.

In Japanese the word for this insect is the same as the word for an old-fashioned straw raincoat. Can you guess why?

But How Do They Make Their Nests?

Larvae hatch from eggs. They make a nest with twigs and dead leaves. They tie them together with threads from their mouths.

▲ Larvae hang on sticky threads from their mouths.

▲ The larva ties bark together with threads.

▲ The nest is now larger. The larva lives inside it.

▲ The larva goes inside the nest and stretches it.

Bagworms ruin bushes and trees by eating leaves and bark.

13

❓ Why Are a Dragonfly's Eyes So Big?

(ANSWER) Dragonflies look for their food during the daytime. It is easier to find with big eyes. Those big eyes also help them watch out for enemies that would catch them. Because they have such big eyes, it is easier to get away.

■ A dragonfly's eye

A dragonfly's eye is made up of many small eyes. Each tiny eye sees almost the same thing. Most insects have the same kind of eye a dragonfly has.

▶ The small eyes come together.

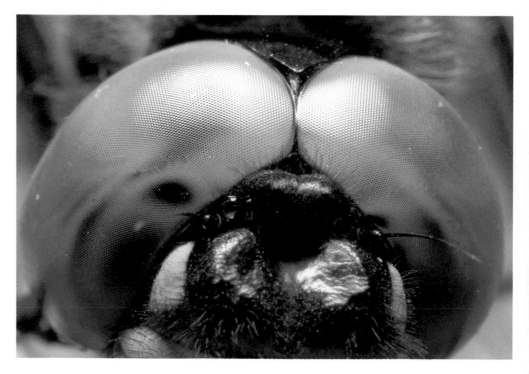

14

Some insects with big eyes

▲ **Horsefly.** Its big eyes shine with the colors of the rainbow.

▲ **Mantis.** It has large eyes in a triangle-shaped face.

▲ **Butterfly.** It has big black eyes.

● To the Parent

Insects' eyes are one of two kinds: small single eyes, or compound ones made up of many small eyes. Compound eyes can detect movement much better than they can make out shapes.

15

❓ Why Does a Dragonfly Dip Its Tail Into the Water?

ANSWER Female dragonflies dip their tails in the water to lay their eggs. Here you see a few of the different kinds of dragonflies. Each type has its own way of laying its eggs in the water.

❓ What Happens After the Eggs Hatch?

Dragonfly nymphs hatch from the eggs. They live and grow in the water. When they reach full size they've turned into dragonflies. They leave the water and fly away.

▲ The dragonfly lays eggs in the water.

▲ The eggs are covered with a thin coating.

▲ A young dragonfly has just hatched.

▲ Young dragonflies are called nymphs. As they grow they shed their old skins many times.

● To the Parent

The female common dragonfly deposits its eggs on water plants while it is connected to the male. Another dragonfly lays eggs by striking the surface of the water with its tail as the male watches above her. The black-winged damselfly rests on water plants and lays eggs on them. Still another species scatters its eggs while it is attached to the male.

17

⍰ Why Do Scarab Beetles Have Horns?

ANSWER Male scarab beetles use their strong horns for fighting. The beetle that throws the other by the horns is the winner. The male beetles don't fight with the females, which have no horns.

Males get ready to fight.

A fight!
A fight!

Male beetles fight by pushing and trying to throw each other out of the way by the horns.

But Why Do They Fight?

They fight over the female.
The stronger male wins her.

Give it to him!

Some beetles also fight over food.
They like the sap of trees very much.
Sometimes they chase away other
kinds of insects that like tree sap.

Get out
of the way!

● **To the Parent**

There are more than 30,000 species of scarab beetles
throughout the world. They range in size from a half
inch to six inches (1-15 cm) long. Males of some species of
scarab beetles are prominently horned. The one illustrated
here is an Oriental variety. But despite their almost
frightening appearance scarab beetles do not harm people.

❓ Why Do Scarab Beetles Die Quickly?

ANSWER All living things die sooner or later — people, animals and insects. Some live longer than others. Adult scarab beetles live only during summer. That is when they lay their eggs. But even after the adults die the eggs will go on living.

Coming out of the ground

Scarab beetles live in the forest in summer. The males find female mates.

Drinking tree sap

Females lay eggs in the ground.

The scarab beetle dies at the end of summer.

A dead beetle

This beetle has a short life. It lives only from one full moon to the next.

■ Hatching scarab beetles live under dead or rotting leaves for about 11 months

That's about the same time it takes for a human baby to start walking.

| Egg | A larva leaves the egg | Larva | Pupa | Emerging adult scarab beetle |

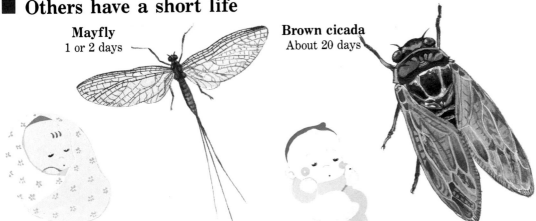

❓ And Do Other Adult Insects Die So Soon?

Some live longer than beetles.
Others have a shorter adult life.

■ Some live a long time

Queen termite
About 25 years

Queen bee
About 5 years

Stag beetle
About 5 years

■ Others have a short life

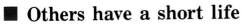

Mayfly
1 or 2 days

Brown cicada
About 20 days

● To the Parent

The life span of a beetle is about a year. Most of that time is spent in the the ground as an egg, a larva and a pupa. Adult beetles emerge from their homes in the ground on summer days and begin their very short lives. After only about a month they die.

❓ **Why Do Some Beetles Have Long Feelers?**

ANSWER Some beetles can't see very well, so they use their feelers to learn what the area around them is like. When they walk they move their feelers around very quickly so that they will go the right way and not run into things. These feelers also help beetles get around at night.

What's this thing?

I smell my favorite tree!

Do Insects with Good Eyes Have Short Feelers?

Yes. Insects with good eyesight usually have short feelers. If their eyes are good enough to find food and spot an enemy, they don't need long feelers.

■ Insects with short feelers are active in daytime

▲ Cicada

▲ Dragonfly

▲ Honeybee

■ Insects with long feelers are active after dark

▲ Katydid

▲ Crickct

▲ Carpenter ant

Why Do Some Beetles Make a Crying Sound?

ANSWER Long-horned beetles make squeaking or crying sounds when you catch them. They are trying to scare you away. If you let them go, they stop making the sounds. Beetles don't make sounds the way birds or people do. They make their crying sounds by rubbing a place between the front and rear halves of their bodies.

Squeak! Squeak!

It's trying to scare you so it can escape.

It makes its cry the same way you make sounds with this instrument.

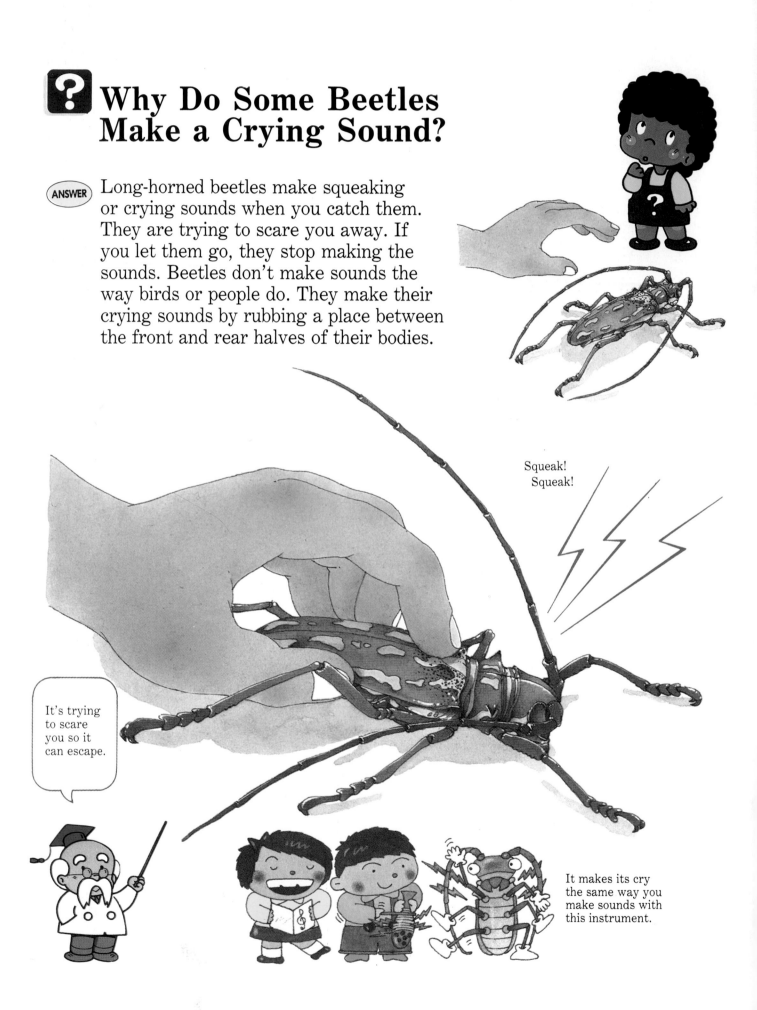

24

And How Do Crickets and Grasshoppers Chirp?

Crickets and grasshoppers make sounds by rubbing their wings together. Locusts rub their back legs and their wings together to make sounds. Only the males of these species make sounds.

▲ **Cricket.** It holds up its wings and rubs them together to make sounds.

▲ **Locust.** It makes sounds by rubbing its back legs and its wings together.

Only the males make sounds.

Band-winged locust
It makes sounds by hitting its wings together while it is flying.

▲ **Grasshopper.** It makes sounds by spreading its wings sideways and rubbing them together.

● **To the Parent**

Long-horned beetles have sound plates between their front and back skins. They rub these plates together to produce sounds. Other types of beetles rub their rear legs against their hard front wings to generate sounds. Crickets and long-horned grasshoppers have right wings that are notched and left wings that are something like files. These insects produce their sounds by rubbing the files along the notches.

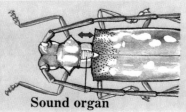

Sound organ

25

Why Do Stag Beetles Have Pincers?

ANSWER Male stag beetles fight with each other over food. They also fight each other to get female mates. And they have to fight to defend themselves against enemies. They need their strong pincers for all that fighting that they must do.

Stag beetle fight
The beetles scare their enemies by opening their pincers and waving them around. They beat their enemies by pinching them with the pincers.

A beetle uses its pincers to defend itself.

And Do Female Stag Beetles Fight Too?

Female stag beetles don't fight. They have only small pincers. The females use their pincers to dig holes. Then they lay their eggs in the holes.

▲ **Female stag beetle.** She has small pincers.

▲ **Male stag beetle.** He has large, strong pincers.

• To the Parent

The beetle's pincers, which look something like scissors, actually are overdeveloped jaws. The males hit each other fiercely with their pincers when they fight over food or females. Usually the beetle that appears to be losing will withdraw quickly, so most fights do not last very long.

MINI-DATA

If you poke the back of a stag beetle with your finger, it gets angry and raises its pincers. If you push harder, the beetle will stretch to reach you. But it will fall over because the pincers are so heavy. It takes the beetle a long time to get up off its back again.

over he goes!

and poke...

If you poke...

Who Is Hiding Here?

(ANSWER) Look very closely at this picture. Do you see the clever moth hiding on the tree? Insects hide from their enemies. Sometimes their color and markings make them very hard to see.

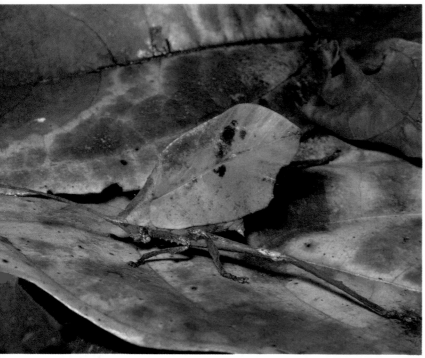

▲ This leaf katydid's markings are almost exactly the same as the leaf it is on. That helps it hide from enemies who might eat it.

▲ This looks just like tree bark, but if you look closely you can see the moth hiding on the tree.

▶ That is a bee on the dandelion. The frog knows that a bee can sting. When it sees the flower fly the frog thinks that it is a bee. While the frog wonders if it is safe for him to eat the flower fly, the flower fly escapes.

▲ This looks like a bee, but it is not. It's a flower fly. The flower fly cannot sting. But other animals think it's a bee, so they leave it alone.

28

How Else Do Insects Fool Their Enemies?

Some insects look like parts of plants. Can you spot the walking stick hiding on this branch?

Blending in with the things around you is called camouflage. Insects are very good at it, but other animals use camouflage for protection too.

● **To the Parent**

Many insects are masters of the fine art of camouflage. They have evolved specific markings and sophisticated behavior, enabling them to blend discreetly into their surroundings. Other insects are mimics. By copying the appearance of more dangerous insects, or by giving the impression of being part of a much larger animal, they attempt to remain safe from potential and real enemies.

This moth has big spots on its wings. To a bird flying nearby, those spots might look like the eyes of a much bigger animal. So the bird is scared and stays away.

29

? Why Do Ladybugs Spit Yellow Liquid When They Are Caught?

ANSWER That yellow liquid is the ladybug's way of protecting itself from its enemies. Put a little bit of it on your fingertip and sniff. It smells terrible, and it tastes even worse. If an insect or bird tries to eat a ladybug once it will not try it the next time. So you can see that this liquid helps keep ladybugs alive.

I'm not going to eat that! It smells terrible!

Whew!
It stinks!

MINI-DATA

Ladybugs flip over on their backs and play dead when other insects and small birds try to catch them. Their enemies are surprised and give up. When it's safe the ladybugs are able to get away.

Oh!
It's dead!

I was only
playing dead!

If you put a ladybug on a pole or bar you'll see that it always walks up to the highest point before it flies away.

❓ Why Do Fireflies Glow?

ANSWER Their tails produce light. When a female flashes her light the male answers by flashing his. It's as though they're calling to each other. That's the way fireflies find mates.

❓ And Do Young Fireflies Also Glow?

Not only the adults glow. Young ones and even the eggs give off a light.

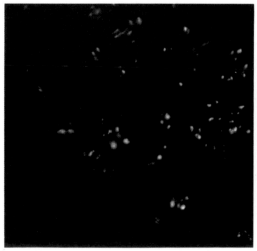

▲ Fireflies' eggs light up the night.

▲ Light glows brightly on the larva.

Even the pupa of the insect shines.

● **To the Parent**

A flashing area can be seen on the rear part of a firefly's tail. A transparent film there covers a large cell that contains substances called luciferin and luciferase. When those come into contact with oxygen, they produce a glowing light. The light does not give off heat, however. The main purpose of the fireflies' flashing lights is to attract mates. Fireflies recognize and respond to each other's flashing lights.

How Do Ants Find Sugar?

ANSWER Ants are always looking for food. They even come into the house for it. Ants love sugar. Any ant that finds some sugar goes back to the nest. As it goes it leaves a trail that other ants can smell. That way the ants in the nest can find their way to where the sugar is.

Food for Ants

Many ants like sweet-tasting food very much.
Some ants eat the dead bodies of other insects.
And some ants eat only fruit and grass.

They eat grass and fruit.

They enjoy spilled drinks.

They love flower nectar.

They like to sip the sweet juice made by aphids.

Sometimes they eat other living things.

■ An ant's nose

The feelers of an ant are its nose. The ant smells things with its feelers. Using the feelers it can tell whether food is good or bad.

● To the Parent

Ants are always looking for food. When they find some, they apply certain body chemicals to the ground as they take part of the food back to the nest. By following this chemical's trail the other ants can go back and forth to the food. They leave their own chemicals on the path and it becomes a major thoroughfare between the nest and the location of the food. Most ants eat anything. Some will even eat meat, but others, such as the black ant, eat nothing but fruits and grasses.

❓ Why Do Ants Touch Each Other With Their Feelers?

ANSWER It is what they do instead of talking. Ants can't make sounds, but they can talk to each other with their feelers. They're saying things like, "I'm hungry" and "I know where there's some good food. Let's hurry and get it."

There's some good food.

Ah, I can smell it. This is the way back to the nest.

You're my sister, aren't you?

36

Ah, food!

I'm taking some back to the others.

Hey! An ant from another nest!

Inside the dark nest the ants' feelers help them find their way without bumping into one another.

● **To the Parent**

Feelers, called antennae, are important sensory organs that ants use to tell one thing from another by smell. Because ants have poor eyesight their antennae play the role that is normally performed by eyes. They are used to identify other ants, to search for food and find the way back to the nest. Ants will battle fiercely to defend their nest and friends, and they will fight just as hard with other ants for food.

? What Is an Ant Nest Like?

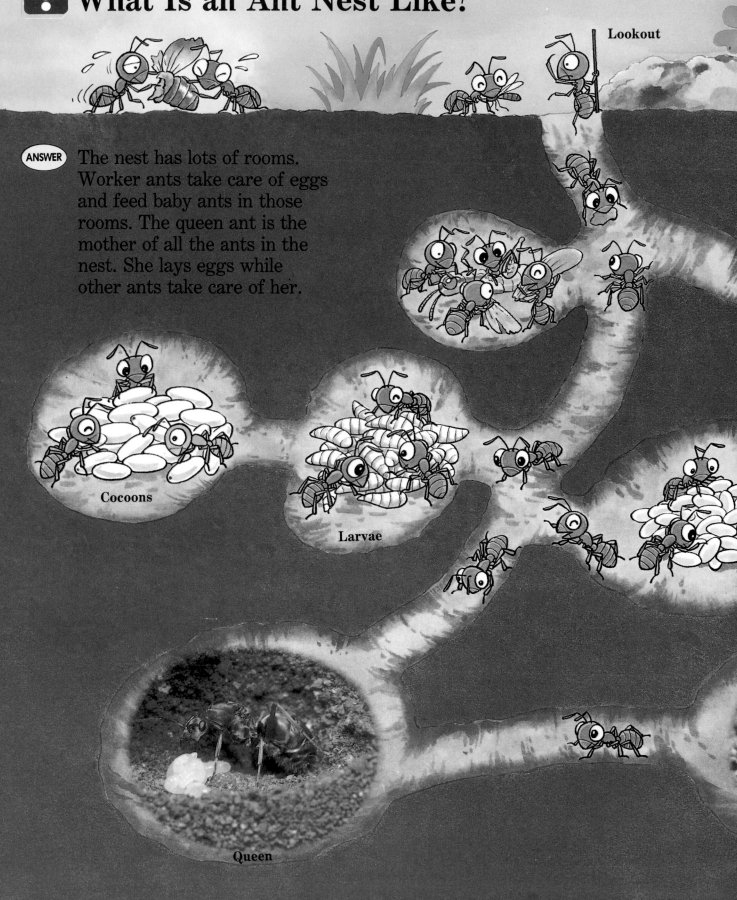

Lookout

ANSWER The nest has lots of rooms. Worker ants take care of eggs and feed baby ants in those rooms. The queen ant is the mother of all the ants in the nest. She lays eggs while other ants take care of her.

Cocoons

Larvae

Queen

Lookout

Eggs

Garbage Pit

Workers caring for baby ants

● To the Parent

Ants' nests have many rooms and interconnecting tunnels. In each nest there is a queen with many worker ants, all of which are her own offspring. When a new queen is born she leaves the nest and flies unprotected until she finds a male of her species. The two mate, then the male ant dies. The queen alights, builds a new nest and starts her own colony.

❓ Why Do Bees Sting?

ANSWER Bees and wasps will sting you if you bother them or their nest. They sting people and animals, and sometimes other insects. They use their stingers to defend their family and nest. Don't annoy them and they won't sting.

There's a bear!
Let's get him!

Oh oh!!
There's
a bear!!

B-z-z-z-z-z

Bees' nests are a big attraction
for some animals. Bears
like honey very much.

Bees team up and fight
together to protect the nest.

Where's the Stinger Located?

A bee's stinger is usually inside its
abdomen. When the bee is ready to sting,
the stinger comes out of its tail.

Getting stung by
a bee must hurt
more than this!

The stinger
comes out
right here.

▲ **Honeybee stinger.** It's usually in the abdomen.

41

How Do Wasps Make Their Nests?

ANSWER Some wasps bite off dead wood, mix it with saliva and make a paste. They fly back and forth to the nest. Each time they add a little paste to the nest until it is finished.

▲ It bites off wood to make paste for building a nest.

As soon as they are born young wasps begin to make a nest. Here the nest has become a fairly large one.

• **To the Parent**

The first nest made by a queen wasp is small and has only one cell. Soon after completing the cell, the queen lays an egg in it, then she makes another cell and lays another egg. In this manner she gradually increases the number of cells. When workers are born, they take over the task of building the nest, and the queen devotes all her time to laying eggs.

▲ The queen wasp uses her mouth to make her first nest.

▲ As soon as the first cell is finished, she lays an egg in it.

▲ She keeps on making cells and lays one egg in each cell. When finished the nest may hold many eggs.

▲ Larvae hatch from the eggs. The queen brings them food, meantime making the nest bigger and bigger.

■ Some other wasps' and bees' nests

▼ **Made of leaves**
Here's a bee's nest made with rose leaves stuffed inside bamboo.

◄ **Made of mud**
This wasp nest is made of mud. When the mud dries out it turns hard.

❓ Did You Know that Honeybees Talk to One Another?

I'll tell everyone.

ANSWER When a honeybee finds a flower with nectar, it goes back to the nest and tells the other bees about it. The bee does a special dance to let the others know where the flower is. For a flower that is nearby, the bee does a simple, round dance. For one that's farther away, it dances in a figure 8. The way the bee dances gives the other bees a good idea of where to go to find the nectar.

Oh, I see. The flower is far from here.

The flower is this way.

▲ **Bees dancing**
The bee that found the flower tells the others where it is.

Here they are! Right here!

▲ **A bee finds the flower.** After watching the dance, most bees can fly straight to the flower.

● **To the Parent**

When a bee finds a flower it returns to the hive and informs the rest of the bees by dancing. If the flower is within 100 yards (90 m) of the hive, the dance is circular. If it is more distant, the dance is a figure-8 pattern. The angle between the center line of the dance and the sun's direction, at the top of the dance pattern, indicates the path to the flower.

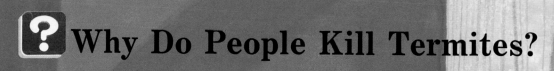

Why Do People Kill Termites?

ANSWER Termites love damp wood. They chew it and make it crumble. They eat away the wood under the floor. Before long the house may even fall down. So people kill termites to save their houses.

Termite queen
She's full of eggs. The queen lays eggs all the time.

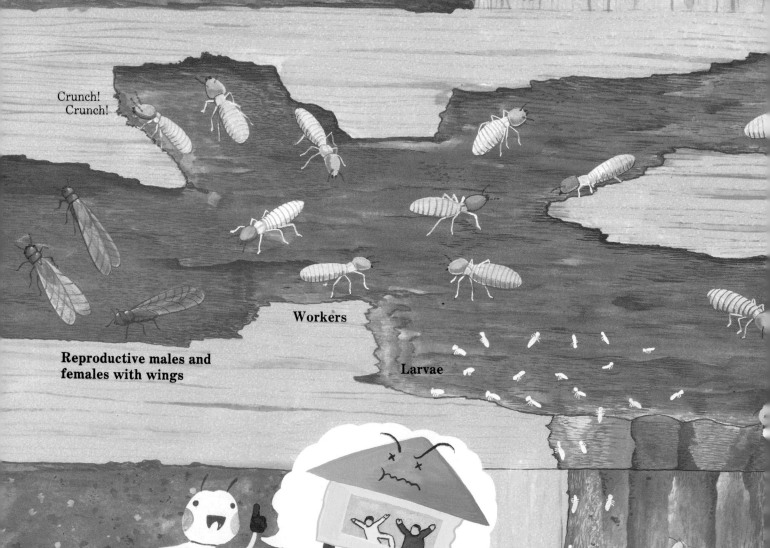

Crunch!
Crunch!

Workers

Reproductive males and females with wings

Larvae

Worker termite taking care of eggs

There's a nest of termites.

Black ants

Enemy!

Soldier termite

Soldier termite

Crunch!
Crunch!

Queen

Workers

Eggs

● **To the Parent**

A termite looks very much like an ant but actually is more closely related to the cockroach. Termites live in families, or colonies. The queen might lay as many as several million eggs during her lifetime. Some termites make new nests in damp wood. The wooden support beams under a house have to be kept dry and well ventilated so that termites will not damage them.

? Why Do Winged Ants Fly?

ANSWER Winged ants mate from spring to summer. The females leave the nest and fly high into the sky. Many males follow them but most can't catch up with the females. As they fly around, lights attract them. That's why they sometimes come into houses during the night.

Ants flying away to mate

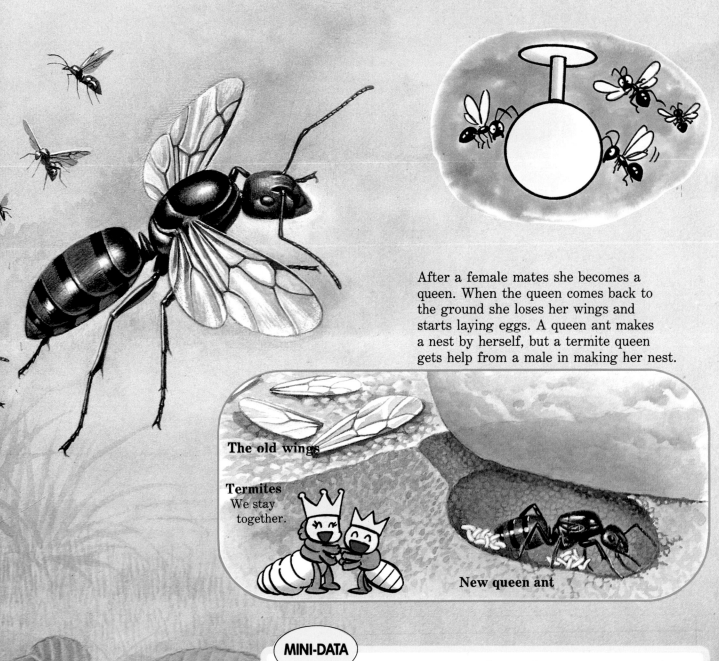

After a female mates she becomes a queen. When the queen comes back to the ground she loses her wings and starts laying eggs. A queen ant makes a nest by herself, but a termite queen gets help from a male in making her nest.

The old wings

Termites
We stay together.

New queen ant

● To the Parent

Both male and female flying ants have wings. During the mating season they leave the nest together in a mating flight. The male that catches up with a female is the only one that can mate with her. Males that do not find mates cannot return to their nests. Unmated males die after a few days. Male and female termites fly out of the nest during the daytime in the early summer. They are called winged ants although they are not true ants.

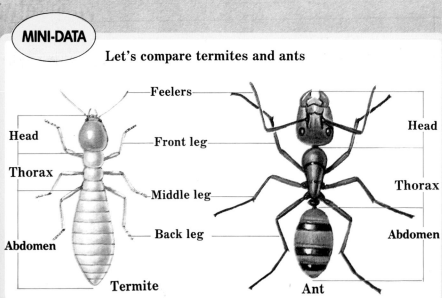

MINI-DATA

Let's compare termites and ants

Feelers

Head

Thorax

Abdomen

Termite

Front leg

Middle leg

Back leg

Head

Thorax

Abdomen

Ant

What Do Praying Mantises Eat?

(ANSWER) Mantises eat only living insects. They never eat dead ones. The front legs of a mantis have spines on them. The spines help hold insects that the mantis has caught. The insects can't escape from the mantis's legs.

I don't eat dead insects.

▼ Mantis eating a drone fly that it has just caught

■ Catching a honeybee

It hides quietly near a flower.

Then it gets ready to spring.

Suddenly it pounces with its front legs.

The prey is finished.

● To the Parent

Mantises are very good at catching insects. They can move their heads up, down and sideways without moving their bodies. Mantises and dragonflies are among the very few insects that have this ability. Other insects do not notice the mantis's slow movements. When catching its prey a mantis draws in its front legs. Then it suddenly extends them and pushes the victim down between the spines on its front legs.

MINI-DATA

Mantises don't use their front legs much when they're walking. They use them to scare away their enemies and to catch the insects they want to eat.

● If someone holds a dead insect in front of it a mantis will think it is alive and will try to catch it.

The mantis walks with its middle and back legs.

❓ Did You Know that Crickets Have Ears?

ANSWER Crickets have ears on their front legs, not on their heads. Their ears help them hear the sounds that other crickets make.

CHIRP!

Here's the cricket's ear.

▲ **A cricket's ear.** It has a film that picks up sound.

Do Other Insects Have Ears Too?

Yes. Insects that make sounds, such as cicadas, long-horned beetles and grasshoppers, can also hear sounds made by insects of their own species.

▲ **Long-horned grasshopper.** It hears sounds with a thin coating on its front legs.

▲ **Migratory locust.** It has a large, thin membrane inside its rear leg joint.

▲ **Cicada.** It hears through a membrane toward the base of its abdomen.

▲ **Honeybee.** It picks up sound with its feelers.

● **To the Parent**

Insects that produce sounds have sensory organs to detect sounds too. Crickets and long-horned grasshoppers have eardrums on their front legs. On both sides of a cicada's abdomen is a film or membrane that functions as an ear. Some grasshoppers have an eardrum on their abdominal area. Honeybees, flies and mosquitoes are able to detect sounds with their feelers.

? How Do Grasshoppers Jump?

ANSWER A grasshopper's back legs are long, thick and strong. Often a grasshopper needs to jump a long distance or to get away from an enemy quickly. It will stretch out its back legs and spring up into the air. Then by flying it can go even farther.

Here comes an enemy!

Legs pulled up to jump.

■ The long jump

This is how far some insects can jump without using wings.

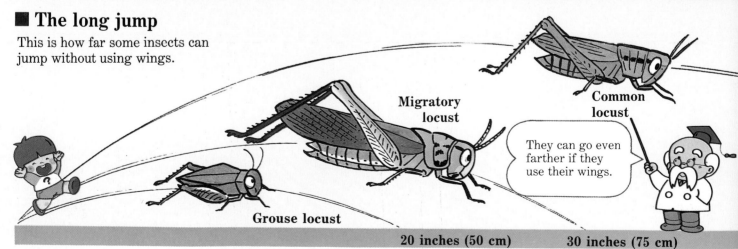

Migratory locust

Common locust

They can go even farther if they use their wings.

Grouse locust

20 inches (50 cm)　　30 inches (75 cm)

I made it!

MINI-DATA

Good swimmers

Grasshoppers can swim by hitting the water with their back legs. Water is no problem for them.

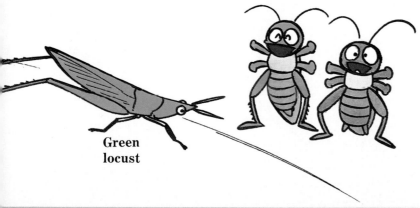

Green locust

5 feet (150 cm)

● To the Parent

Migratory locusts lay their eggs in the ground in the autumn. By about May of the following year the nymphs hatch and come up out of the ground. At this stage they are shaped like adults, but they have no wings. As they grow their wings develop, and the young locusts shed their skin, or molt, several times. By the summertime they become adults with fully developed wings.

Why Do Mole Crickets Have Big Legs?

ANSWER Mole crickets live underground. They have large, thick front legs for digging. They move through the ground by making tunnels. They can push the soil out of the way quickly with their big, thick legs.

She protects her eggs.

■ A mole cricket's life

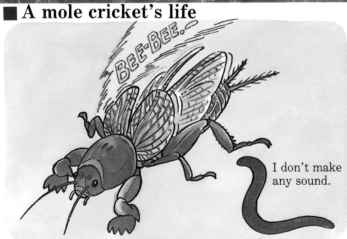

BEE-BEE-!

I don't make any sound.

Males and females make sounds.

If an enemy attacks, they shoot out a smelly juice.

56

Don't come out!
There's a bird out here!

They eat grass roots.

They eat earthworms.

They're good swimmers.

They come out of the ground at night.
Sometimes they fly toward light.

Why Can Water Striders Walk on the Water?

Because water striders are so light, they can stand on the water with their long legs. At the end of each leg there are lots of fine, thin hairs. The hairs are waterproof, so the water strider doesn't sink.

▲ The end of the leg is hairy.

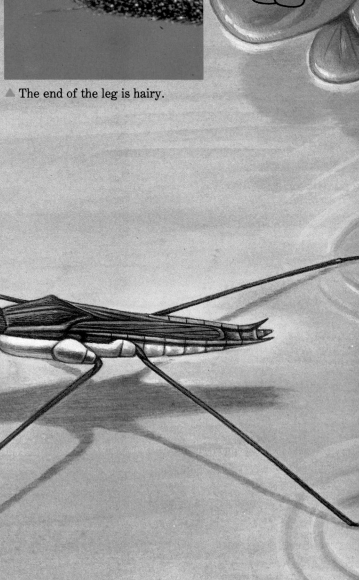

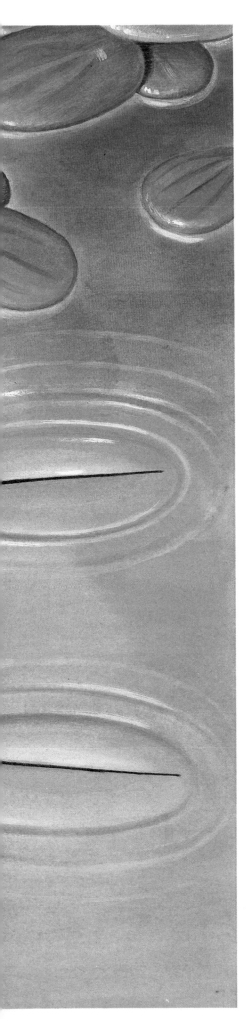

 # Just How Do They Catch Their Food?

Water striders stand on their
four long legs. There are two
in the middle and two in back.
They use two short front legs
to catch insects that fall into
the water. They have beaks
like needles, and when they
catch insects they suck out
the juices with their beaks.

TRY THIS

If you very carefully put a
light, flat piece of aluminum
on water it will float. That
is because there is a thin film
on the surface of the water. It
keeps the metal from sinking.
Water striders move around on this
film, and it keeps them afloat.

⊛ **To the Parent**

The water strider moves with a sort of skating motion on water,
taking advantage of what is known as surface tension. Fine
hairs on the insect's feet repel the water and help keep the
insect afloat. The ends of its thin legs are angled sideways
so they do not break through the film on the water's surface.

❓ What Are These Strange Things?

It's hard!

■ Mantis egg case

This is a mantis's egg case with lots of eggs inside. In the spring the nymphs all come out at one time.

■ Weevil cradle

This is the cradle of a leaf-rolling weevil. The weevils make cradles by wrapping leaves together. Then they lay eggs in them.

■ Spittlebug nest

This is a spittlebug nest. Young spittlebugs live by covering themselves with little bubbles.

What monsters!

■ Cicada shells

These are shells of skin the cicadas have left behind. Young cicadas grow up in the ground. When they come out of the ground they climb out of their old skin and leave the shell.

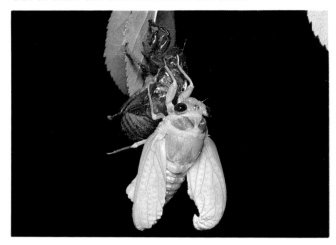

■ Walking stick eggs

These are the eggs of a flying walking stick. The insect lives in trees where it lays its eggs. The eggs fall to the ground.

What are those things?

■ Ground spider nest

The ground spider's nest is half buried and half above ground.

That's my house.

• To the Parent

Cast-off skins of cicadas are found during the spring and summer. Leaf-rolling weevils make cradles on garden roses. Mantis egg cases are found in open fields and gardens, and sometimes under the eaves in the winter. Walking-stick eggs lie on the ground and look like fruit. Ground-spider nests are seen on places like tree roots, stone walls and fences.

61

❓ Why Do Only Female Mosquitoes Bite?

ANSWER The females suck blood from people and animals. They need it to help them lay eggs. If they don't drink blood, most mosquitoes can't lay eggs. So they stick their mouth, like a needle, into people and animals and suck up blood. Males suck up only water and plant juices.

Males drink the juices of fruit, trees and leaves.

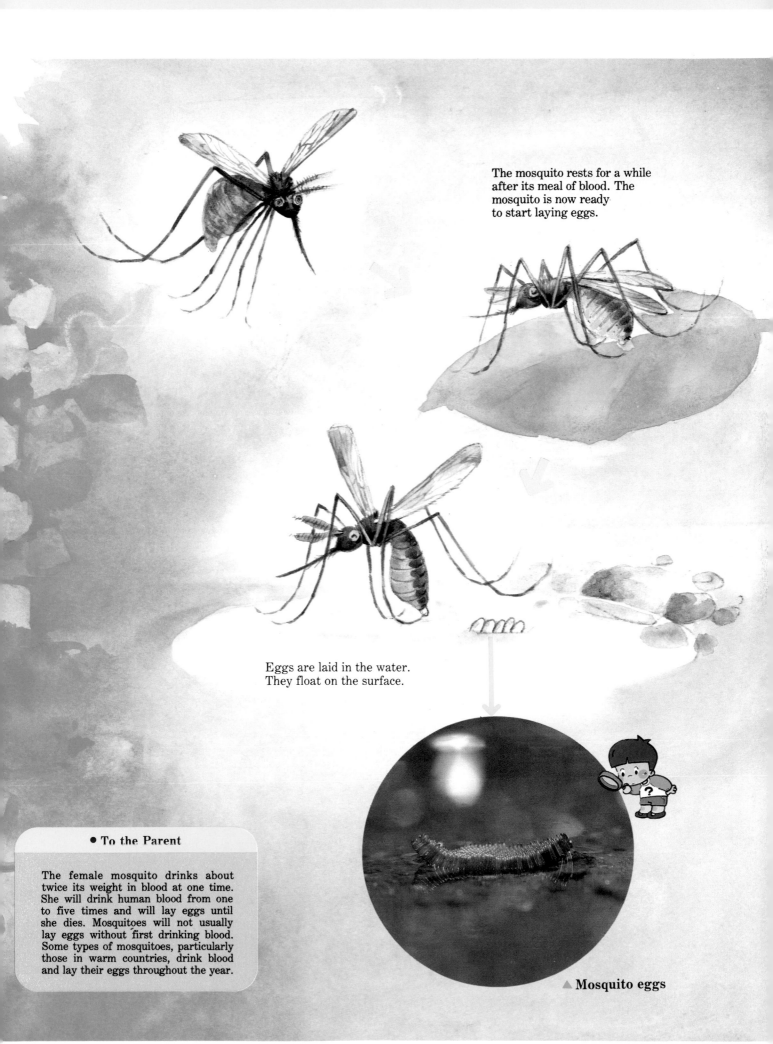

The mosquito rests for a while after its meal of blood. The mosquito is now ready to start laying eggs.

Eggs are laid in the water. They float on the surface.

● To the Parent

The female mosquito drinks about twice its weight in blood at one time. She will drink human blood from one to five times and will lay eggs until she dies. Mosquitoes will not usually lay eggs without first drinking blood. Some types of mosquitoes, particularly those in warm countries, drink blood and lay their eggs throughout the year.

▲ Mosquito eggs

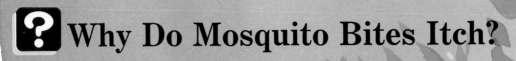

Why Do Mosquito Bites Itch?

ANSWER Mosquitoes bite people and drink their blood. When they drink the blood they mix in some of their own saliva. That helps them drink it more easily. The saliva is what makes your skin itch.

■ A mosquito drinking blood

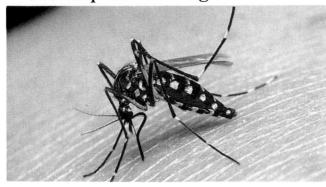

▲ It sticks its mouth in, adds saliva and drinks blood.

▲ It sucks steadily for a while and gets a big stomach.

64

Mosquitoes Live in Places Like These

■ Where some blood drinkers live

Around houses

Inside houses

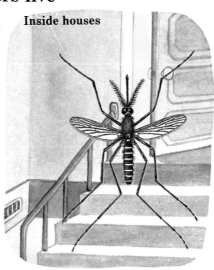

Inside farm buildings

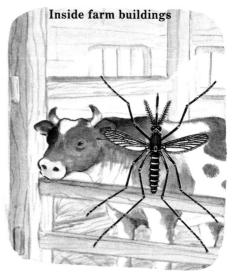

In bamboo groves

In woodlands

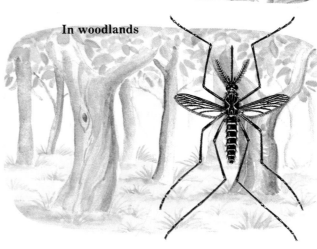

■ Some that don't drink blood

I'm not a mosquito.

Crane fly

Midge

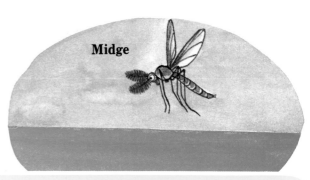

● **To the Parent**

Mosquitoes can transmit diseases, such as encephalitis and malaria. Disease-causing organisms often enter the mosquito when it drinks blood and then are transmitted in the saliva released by the insect when it pierces another victim's skin. Mosquitoes can be eliminated by getting rid of the wet places where they breed, such as swamps, old cans or pools of water.

❓ Why Does Everyone Hate Cockroaches?

ANSWER Cockroaches give off an oil that smells bad. But worse than that, cockroaches are often found in dirty places. They carry lots of germs on their feet and bodies. Cockroaches walk on dishes and food with their dirty feet. The germs they leave behind can be harmful to people.

A Cockroach's Strange Body

▼ It can run very fast.

▲ It can squeeze into very narrow cracks.

▼ Some kinds of cockroaches can even fly!

▲ It has feelers that can pick up sounds.

A cockroach's strange life

▼ Some of them lay 30 to 40 eggs at a time and put them into a case like a wallet.

If you see one cockroach, you can bet that there are many others nearby.

▼ They like to live close together in small, narrow spaces.

▼ They become most active after the sun goes down.

It's time to get to work.

● To the Parent

The common black cockroach, the kind you see in the kitchen, lays 20 to 25 eggs in a case about a half inch (12 mm) long. In about 40 days the eggs hatch. As the wingless nymphs grow they shed their skin repeatedly. They do not reach adulthood until the following summer. Cockroaches normally begin to move around when the sun sets and are most active at night.

How Can Flies Stand Upside-Down on the Ceiling?

ANSWER At the ends of flies' feet there are sharp claws and lots of sticky hairs. The claws and hairs help flies hold onto the ceiling when they're upside-down. Because their bodies are very light, it's easier for them to hold on without falling.

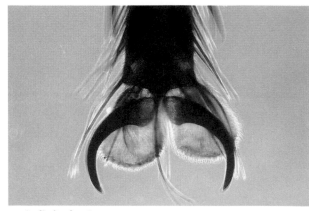

▲ A fly's foot

Flies can hang onto the ceiling with their feet. It's easy for them to hold on even when they're upside-down.

With the hair on their feet they can even hold onto glass.

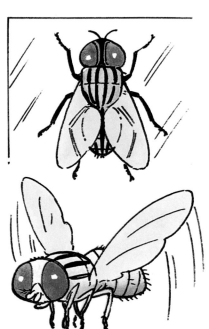

Some others that don't fall

A jumping spider

At the ends of this spider's feet there are bunches of hairs that are like suckers.

A ladybug

The white places on a ladybug's feet have suckers.

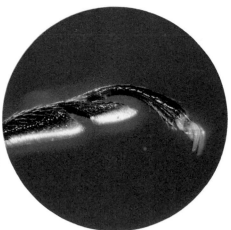

A Fly's Body

It picks up smells with its short feelers. They act like a nose.

It has lips that are like sponges at the end of its mouth.

Here are the hairs.

It uses the hairs on its feet to find out how something tastes.

It can fly away very quickly.

A gecko's foot

There are suckers on each toe on the lizard's foot.

● **To the Parent**

Jumping spiders, flies, gecko lizards and some other animals can cling to ceilings and walk on vertical glass. The secret is in the feet and is visible under a microscope. We can see suckers, claws or a thick growth of sticky hair on the feet. With their special equipment any number of spiders, lizards and other insects can crawl on ceilings and glass with ease.

❓ Why Do Spiders Spin Webs?

ANSWER Spiders eat only living things. They spin webs and wait for insects to get caught in them. A web is a trap to catch insects for food, and it is also the spider's home. When an insect gets caught in the web, the spider hurries to it. The insect tries to get away, but the spider rolls it up in sticky threads. Then it kills the insect with poison and has it for dinner.

Spiders are arachnids, not insects, but since they are very much involved with the insect world, which they feed on, we have included them in this book.

Why Aren't Spiders Caught in Their Own Webs?

A spider's web has two kinds of threads in it. The ones that make a spiral or circle pattern are sticky. The other threads are not. Those are the ones that the spider walks on. That is why he does not get caught.

This thread is sticky.

This one is not.

▲ Spider's foot ▲ Spider's thread

Some spiders don't make webs

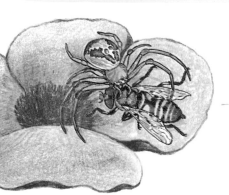

▲ **Flower spider**
Hides near flowers and jumps out to catch flying insects. It jumps out and attacks quickly.

▲ **Jumping spider**
Finds insects by walking around in the grass and trees.

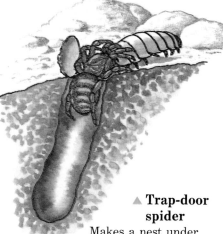

▲ **Trap-door spider**
Makes a nest under the ground, then jumps out and catches insects.

▲ **Wolf spider**
Walks around on the ground and catches insects. It also gets insects that fall into water.

• To the Parent

At the tip of a spider's abdomen are special organs called spinnerets, which produce mucus. When the mucus comes into contact with air, it becomes thread. To make webs, spiders spin threads of different thicknesses and types. The threads are almost as strong as nylon threads of the same thickness.

❓ Why Do Snails Carry Their Houses On Their Backs?

ANSWER Snails live inside shells. The shells are made of the same kind of material as the shells of oysters and clams. The snail's heart, lungs and all other important parts are inside the shell. If the shell is broken the snail can usually fix it. But if it is broken badly and the snail cannot fix it, the animal usually dies.

■ Inside a snail shell

Eye

Lungs

Stomach

Heart

Mout

Bowels

Kidney

Liver

Foot

They're like us!

Snails are actually mollusks, not insects. But since you see them so often you should know about them.

Shells are very important for protecting snails. Snails will die if their bodies get too dry. If they feel that this is about to happen, they go back into their shells and close the opening with a thin film that keeps moisture inside.

Oh, I feel so dry.

This film over the opening keeps the snail from drying out.

Hey, come out!

■ The snail's shell spirals

An adult snail has more spirals than a baby snail has.

I'm an adult!

▲ A snail that's just hatched has only about one and a half spirals.

▲ Two months later the snail has grown and now has three spirals.

? Why Do Snails and Slugs Leave A Shiny Trail?

ANSWER When snails and slugs move about they put out a sticky fluid from the bottom of their foot. The fluid helps them hold onto things. They can even hold onto glass. When the fluid dries it has a silver color and looks sort of shiny.

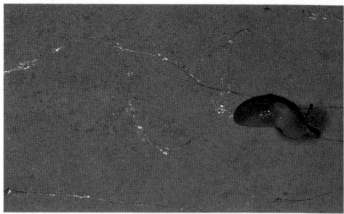

▲ A slug leaves a trail as it crawls.

You're better at holding on than I am!

That's the way to go!

A Snail Circus

▲ Slugs can walk on a spider's thread. They move forward by twisting the thread so that it will hold their heavy bodies.

▲ It can climb to the tip of a head of barley.

▲ A snail is so light it can rest on chestnut spines.

? What Do Earthworms Eat?

ANSWER They eat soil. There are many dead leaves and tiny animals in the soil, and these get mixed with the soil that the earthworms eat. The soil passes through their bodies and goes back into the earth. This makes the ground better for farmers' crops. Worms also put air into the soil, and that also makes it rich. Farmers like earthworms because of this.

An earthworm enjoys a nice dead leaf.

Munch, munch!

Earthworms are actually annelids, but we have put them in the insect book for you.

FERTILIZER

Waste left by earthworms helps plants grow.

Worms' Strange Bodies

Earthworms don't have eyes, but their whole body can sense light.

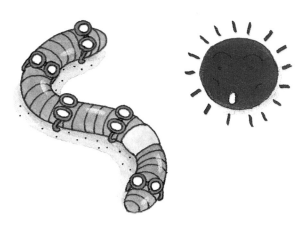

They breathe through their skin. If water gets into their holes, they must come up for air.

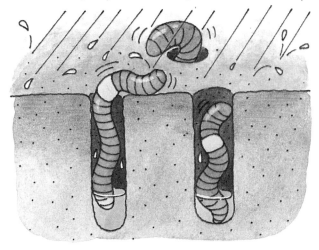

If earthworms can't get back to their underground holes, they will dry out in the sun and die.

There are short hairs on their body to keep them from slipping.

An earthworm that loses its tail can grow a new tail.

● To the Parent

An earthworm stays in its hole in the daytime. At night it partly emerges to eat decaying organic matter close to the entrance to its hole. When the worm's head is at the bottom of the hole it eats the soil there. With its tail outside the hole it leaves droppings that are a natural fertilizer. Earthworms moving through the ground make many holes that let more air and water into the soil and help plants grow.

77

❓ What Are They Doing?

▲ This ant is drinking the sweet juice that comes from the tail of an aphid. In return for the juice the ants protect the aphids. They chase away ladybugs, which will eat aphids.

▲ This wood louse is protecting itself by rolling its body into a ball. Its back is covered by a hard shell.

▲ This measuring worm, or inchworm, hides by pretending to be a twig. This usually fools the worm's enemies.

▲ There's a bubble on this diving beetle's tail. It forms when the beetle breathes out air under water.

▲ A female water bug lays eggs on the back of a male.
The male takes care of the eggs until they hatch.

Water bug fathers have a big job.

● To the Parent

In return for the sweet fluid they drink from aphids, ants protect the aphids from ladybug predators. Practically all diving beetles keep air between their wings and back, and use it to breathe under water. The bubble contains exhaled air. During the maturation period of water-bug eggs the male protects them against enemies.

❓ What's This?

A baby spider gets ready to fly away with the wind

The young spider spins a thread from its tail.
Then it hangs by the thread and waits for the wind.
When the wind comes, it carries the spider away.

A wasp throws water out of its nest

When the nest gets wet because of the rain, this is the way the wasp dries it out.

● To the Parent

Young spiders stay together for a while after they are born. But before long each spins a thread, floats it in the air and drifts away with the thread trailing in the wind. If it becomes too hot inside the wasp's nest, the wasp cools it down by using its wings as fans to blow air into the nest.

80

Growing-Up Album

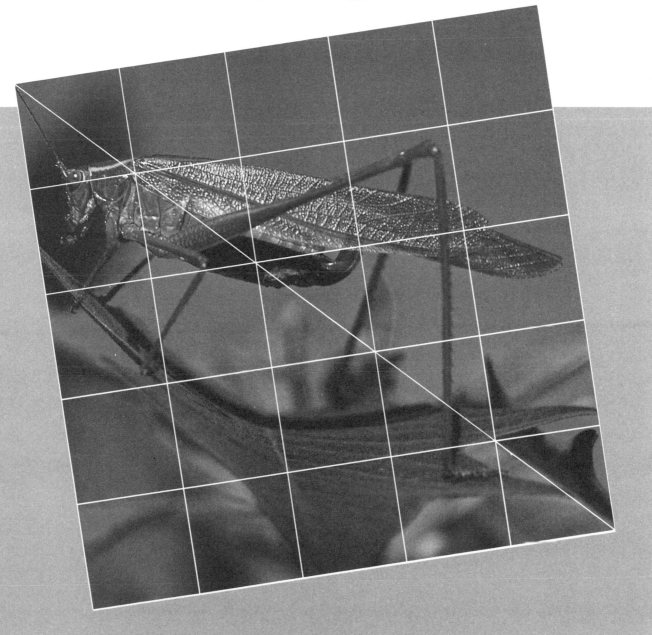

Looking for Insects

Children are attracted to things that move and crawl. They will discover such creatures as insects, frogs and crayfish. Young children do not mind holding a hairy caterpillar, but they may become squeamish about it as they grow older. You can recall some happy memories later if you keep a record here of insects and other tiny creatures that your children have discovered.

An explorer's scrapbook
(sketch or photo)

■ Your children's discoveries

■ Which of these living things did your children find, and how old were they at the time?

Butterflies

Age

Beetles

Age

Wood lice

Age

Snails

Age

Hairy caterpillars

Age

Frogs

Age

■ What else did they discover?

Age	Item

Living Things

An important part of children's development comes
from caring for living things, from small insects
to pet dogs and cats. Providing such care helps
children develop responsibility, a curious mind and
a respect for smaller or weaker creatures. The stronger
a child's powers of observation the more questions he
or she might ask a parent. Record some of them here.

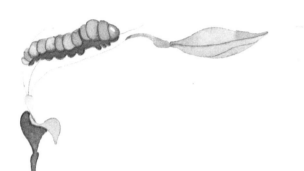

Photographs

■ Questions

■ Which pets have your children raised?

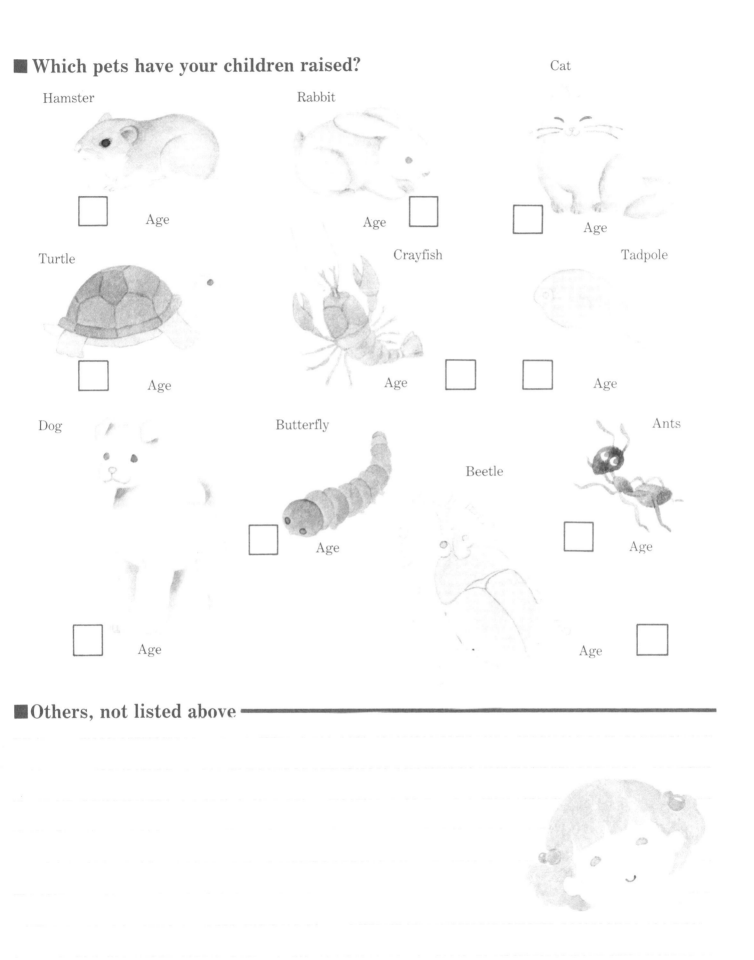

Hamster

☐ Age

Rabbit

Age ☐

Cat

☐ Age

Turtle

☐ Age

Crayfish

Age ☐

Tadpole

☐ Age

Dog

☐ Age

Butterfly

☐ Age

Beetle

Age ☐

Ants

☐ Age

■ Others, not listed above

Who Is Talking?

At the top of these pages are things that different animals might say. On the bottom of the pages are the animals. Do you know who is saying each thing? Draw a line from each animal to what it would say if it could talk.

1.
I have eight legs and live in a web.

2.
I do a special dance to show my friends in the hive where a flower is.

3.
I lay eggs in the water. When my babies are hatched they are called nymphs.

4.
My tail end produces light. I use it to help find a mate.

5.
I use my strong back legs to help me jump away from my enemies.

6.
I bite people and suck their blood. The blood helps me lay my eggs.

Dragonfly

Mosquito

Butterfly

Bee

Snail

Grasshopper

7.
The sharp claws and sticky hairs on my feet help me stand upside-down on the ceiling without falling.

8.
I use my horns to fight other males like me. We fight over females and food.

9.
To protect myself from birds I spit out smelly yellow juice.

10.
I'm not a butterfly even though I look like one. I like to fly around bright lights at night.

11.
I carry my home wherever I go. My shell keeps my body from drying out.

12.
I fly to flowers to collect nectar. When the weather gets cold some insects like me fly south for the winter.

Spider

Scarab beetle

Fly

Firefly

Ladybug

Moth

A Child's First Library of Learning

Insect World

Time-Life Books Inc. is a wholly owned subsidiary of
Time Incorporated.
Time-Life Books, Alexandria, Virginia
Children's Publishing

Director:	Robert H. Smith
Associate Director:	R. S. Wotkyns III
Editorial Director:	Neil Kagan
Promotion Director:	Kathleen Tresnak
Editorial Consultants:	Jacqueline A. Ball
	Andrew Gutelle

Editorial Supervision by:
International Editorial Services Inc.
Tokyo, Japan

Editor:	C. E. Berry
Editorial Staff:	Nobuko Abe
	Christine Alaimo
Design:	Kim Bolitho
Writer:	Winston S. Priest
Editorial Assistants:	Laurie Hanawa
	Janette Bryden
Translation:	Ronald K. Jones

Library of Congress Cataloging in Publication Data
Insect world.
    p.   cm. — (A Child's first library of learning)
    Summary: Presents, in question and answer format,
information about the behavior, food-gathering, defenses,
anatomy, and surprising habits of all kinds of insects.
    ISBN 0-8094-4841-6.   ISBN 0-8094-4842-4 (lib. bdg.)
    1. Insects—Miscellanea—Juvenile literature.
[1. Insects—Miscellanea.   2. Questions and answers.]
I. Time-Life Books.   II. Series.
QL467.2.I57 1988   595.7—dc19   88-20163
©1988 Time-Life Books Inc.
©1983 Gakken Co. Ltd.

Sixth printing. Printed in U.S.A.
Published simultaneously in Canada.

TIME-LIFE is a trademark of Time Incorporated U.S.A.